MASSES

ON

RADAR

MASSES
ON
RADAR

DAVID O'MEARA

COACH HOUSE BOOKS, TORONTO

first edition

Published with the generous assistance of the Canada Council for the Arts and the Ontario Arts Council. Coach House Books also acknowledges the support of the Government of Canada through the Canada Book Fund and the Government of Ontario through the Ontario Book Publishing Tax Credit.

LIBRARY AND ARCHIVES CANADA CATALOGUING IN PUBLICATION

Title: Masses on radar / David O'Meara.
Names: O'Meara, David, author.
Description: Poems.
Identifiers: Canadiana (print) 20210256117 | Canadiana (ebook) 2021025615X | ISBN 9781552454268 (softcover) | ISBN 9781770566767 (EPUB) | ISBN 9781770566774 (PDF)
Classification: LCC PS8579.M359 M37 2021 | DDC C811/.54—dc23

Masses on Radar is available as an ebook: ISBN 978 1 77056 676 7 (EPUB); ISBN 978 1 77076 677 4 (PDF)

Dorothy Jeffreys, ever, always

CONTENTS

1

2

3

4

1

I INVITE BAD LUCK AND RUIN

A god is in the porch.

Dislodged by lawn chairs,
glimpsed in the balustrade,

unbowed by the saturated stomp
of the downpour.

•

It rappels down strands
as tensile as catgut, horsehair,
or Egyptian reeds,

leg over legs,

poised, modelling
its profile for Nazca,
an ancestor's rictus nestled in amber,

like a miser's tie pin,
a crone's brooch

I lift and admire, with a jeweller's tact.

•

I trap it in plastic, some takeout container.
I'm plotting to ogle it.

I didn't read the signs
that hang on a breeze,
though the portents

have told me that touching anything
would mean
I'd become part of it.

•

It skulks the chafed lid, notes
dimensions, a mastermind
clanging its cup on the cage,
testing the thin perimeter.

I leave it for hours
under the sun's white pinwheel.

•

Forgotten, the blot lies puckered,
a false eyelash, weightless,
pinched
at the dry aorta,
curled around itself,
saving its death mask for Paradise.

And the cobweb, found in a joist bay:

silk threads now slack
as batten,

                    frizzed hub
collapsed and clinging
like a guest thrown out on a doorstep.

I CARRY A MOUSE TO THE PARK BESIDE THE HIGHWAY

I couldn't smash its quick life

or leave it
under the hammer-slap
of a metal wire,
that poor change purse of bones

who'd jingled for crumbs on our kitchen counter

all summer
from a station behind the stove
where no one could reach through a dime-sized hole.

•

I portioned the aged cheddar, and
unsnapping the lid of the trap
rigged with a humane, weight-triggered, one-way ramp,
placed the bait inside.

•

Wrapped in a jacket before dawn,
I forced myself to be
a silhouette.
                    In sneakers
I rented thirty minutes from time.
I lifted the tin palanquin,
quivering mouse inside, its brief flight

a bumped spirit level
across vacant intersections
too early for joggers.

•

Since each hour's a sickle with a fighting chance,
I tested fate's etiquette

and flattered the cat's mercy.

I was thinking of the grass's traffic
as I tipped the trap over
between thin shoulder and scissoring headlights,
near park gates
where the mouse's paws typed
their way
through a looping scribble of tomato vines,

while all that hour, the sun's seeping bleach
became a chandelier,
and I turned for home, the morning's alarms,
the news, wage,
      and email, no less

no more.

DISTANT

Our earliest memories are hearsay, or Mom's, the one
reliable witness. Most begin at floor level, before
grammar: table legs, linoleum, toddler push toy

stalled at the carpet trim. Horse's mouth says
I used to chew the verandah's pine doorframe.
Or was that my sister? It's contrapuntal, to exist and also
recall. A trade between turmoil and rest, as any snowglobe

needs wrist-shaken Richters at the onset, then to be placed
on a stable shelf to let grace fall. The lamp before bed
delays dervish remorse. But we must reckon with
a distant image of ourselves, sprawled and blubbing

that the dog bit us. Night birthed the Fates, morning
the milk carton. Tell me, can anyone say where one
self fails and another begins?   (*crickets*)

AHEAD

What good is the future if you can't explain
the future? Maybe you live through it, or experiment with
escape. Go back. Bad dinners, fistfights in August darkness,

rust-coloured drapes, shabby dumpster chairs,
my years sleeping beneath the poster of a blue gargoyle:
REM's *Chronic Town*. What good's the present? The present's
wildfires, genocide, the orangutan

almost extinct. *Stay here*, we plead inside it.
But money has no ears. Wait and we'll see. Same
old. Anger. Unrest. It'll get
louder. Politicians appease, their speeches empty

and thin as an envelope. Ahead, a weird light,
at least. The landfill will outlast the luxury,
day dangled between panic and panic.

I SURF THE SODIUM LIGHT

Shit happens at night without us.
In the hedge, branches dip and click.
Darkness's sleeve
pours forth along the curb,

slight of light,
scored by wind gusts,

itinerant
across a porcelain silence.

•

The snowdrift rests
near the lake's black slab,
guarding its domain in a streetlight's warped pull.

On closed circuit, a fox skates, stitching a trail of prints
across the white contours.
The owl drags its claw like a grapple
toward it, but the shadow
doesn't stab,

snipping its descent
out of an agitated gusting of feathers.

Curious, hungry, the fox bows
and circles. Carnivore do-si-do, cringing, hissing,
but no contact, and no audio

captured. Each doubts
the menace is worth the meal,

shrugs and exits, their
parley's only evidence
snow-punched divots
sunk in the unploughed sidewalk.

•

Mindless, the drift accumulates, rises
like a white loaf.
The cold holds houses like cubes in a tray.

Porches glow, grottoes
to a northern idol,
witness to Cobourg's gentrified harbour,
Europe too busy to notice,
the Nasdaq totally elsewhere.

PUZZLE

Was that you shitposting on Twitter, or worse, rolling
out an inspirational meme? Cleave to the sticky path between.
More feeling, less emoticon. Better a bag of lemons than

Febreze. Or stand back. Find some perspective. Go outside, go
swimming, for fuck's sake. I'm no danger junkie, but a spell
with a mountainside and carabiner would put some vitamin D
in your stride. Wear sunscreen, please. (Also, note Everest mishaps).

Maybe a crossword puzzle is more your speed. Or jigsaw.
Knitting? Death is everywhere. Hobbies are projective, eerie, existential.
In Nagaland, the winner ate fourteen ghost peppers in the chili-eating
contest, then went knock-kneed and glassy-eyed, found fetal

against a wall for the post-game interview. He spoke little English
but managed to convey his state: 'Very no.' Props
for essence. Me, I keep one eye open and one eye closed.

Contra the self-help guide: sweat the small stuff and don't
think outside the box. Think inside the house, its brick
and Tyvek wrap, double-glazed windows, screen

doors, and gable flashing. How it shelters our life
needs steady vigour with mop, baking soda, vinegar,
hard bristles, J Cloth, dustpan, Dyson, and in special cases, tung oil,
caulking, or plunger. Through the hardware store's turnstiles,

you're always forgetting something. Exit, pursued
by a toilet brush. Meanwhile, back at the sty, a Roomba's
let loose in the living room, ramming baseboards with puny rushes,
a feeble vision of the future, proof our domestic AI

is no Rutger Hauer, soon to be laughed at but grimly
muttering *I've seen cat hair you people wouldn't believe*
into the dustbin of, like, literally, the kitchen.

Everything is going to take more money
than expected, I should have known.
I should have known there's no such thing

as a free quote. After the gate crash, it's
bargain bins or shopper-aggro for two
extra inches of HD.
Civilization. We live here, the way

the cat storms the kitchen when a can
is opened. Last week they found
one hundred plastic cups, twenty-five plastic bags,
and two flip-flops inside the stomach of a dead

sperm whale. Billboards promise 'Increased Returns.'
Trapped inside the orange-coned
lane reduction, I'm just shoulder-checking for an exit.

The front path's cruel from freezing rain,
a slick shell.
                    Footfalls
rummage through crust.

I scrape the windshield, splitting ice
to fractions, gouging

frost's derma
into gaps over the passenger view

where he crouches inside his plastic bubble,

green eyes scanning through air holes
                    at my assembling face.

•

The stop sign's
an easel gazing south to vistas cropped

below the Queensway.
Lowry-grim maybe, but peopleless
near Pizza Shark.

A floating eye. A sun-sucked underpaint.

I hunt a passage
through this mid-sized city,

                              coffee thick as pastry
while we stew in the northbound bottleneck.

I can't stay either. I won't go. Not yet,
                              not just now
anyway,

still pinned to the risk of taking care of things.

●

The balance is wrong.
Or petty,

like waking to a world of stolen bicycles.

We try to avoid dawn,
but radiance
rushes at the corners.

●

Road salt collects, chews
at concrete,

and bronzes the tire wells with rust.

With Pantene lustre, two crows
crown the snowbank,

their calls a raucous schtick.

•

The sun is shining on us.
Every corner gleams.
    I go a long while

not expecting anything, then find myself
surprised
at what I feel

and jealous of everything I touch.

I REPLACE KOROTKI AT THE WEATHER STATION ON THE BARENTS SEA

It will stay like this:

filigreed with frost, windows
brim in each retina.
They glom on mute noon's
plum horizon
above snow and shelf edge.

It glows to Svalbard, gets grey,
with no foghorn.

•

Purse seine. Pelagic trawl.

Bejewelled with
an auroral side ridge,

                  capelin
spawn in shore sand,
          flaunt larval drift
and a catch rule.

Alone is only
          no one else now.
Near grass flats, I float a dory punched
with rivets
and scrape mud from treads
on the bucktails,

                    bunched collar in my fist, puffing
the balance of a tobacco ration.

Now I row, no oarlock
and prepared for lag, a scruffy speck
                    lording over the landspit.

•

On duckboards of permafrost,
across sedge and tundra grass,
                  in hip boots, I heave
a tidal marker to shore. Bergs

stall in the opal monochrome.
It stays like so,
all squint

and radar, January gust spanking
the back window. I write *my life is wind*
and post the note
                to nowhere

until summer's supply ship
swans through sea ice.

•

Everything accrues.
I didn't come here hoping.

I called for certain information.

The snowsquall
hallucinates me; its horizontal
crosshatch of low pressure

flails over kindling,
a shovel,
        dog grave, and a dark barn

riding out the epoch.

Behind the altar, the corpse tilts its chin
into a cavity above the ribcage.
Pinned to the folded hands, a Victorian silk ribbon
with brittle pleats.

Dust, once human skin, or maybe
a martyr's toenail,
hangs like desiccated stars
in angled sun by the eastern apse.
All bets are off
when you stand before the mortal vitrine.
Rot makes havoc
with our molecules; blood
fluxes back to powder, encrusting the ampoule.

•

Instead, there's a sponge for your *posca*.
A Holy Lance letter opener.
Replica sandals of Christ.
I falter in the gift shop, and doubt,
and cannot stick
a finger to the proof.

On Via dei Tribunali, tomatoes and arugula.
Between balconies of laundry, the sun's
a cropped monstrance, until a cloud
mops up the light the way
bread does for *la scarpetta*. I pause

over cobblestone, mopeds in succession,
the chapel's swept entry guarded by wrought-iron,
a bronze skull shiny from the repeated rub of fingertips

but no miracle or luck forthcoming.

Someone's gouged the parietal,
its coronal suture a makeshift ashtray.

Inside, the saint's femur glows.
It will not raise you
to heaven any more than a sleigh and a Santa hat
will bring a gift-wrapped toy. The mystic I was
died in velour and feathered bangs
while the cynic is just getting warmer.

Back home, a skin colour will get you shot.
Over there, a drone strike on the wedding feast.

Memento vitae. Down the granite steps,
bishops' bones lie jumbled in the crypt.
Anyone with six euros may enter.

2

Aboard the hydrofoil to Ischia I remembered
I promised to take nothing for granted.

Unfocused or spellbound, I'd missed the stop at Forio,
under a sky wide and luminous as the Mediterranean.

The pending days you couldn't count or waste.
I recalled them again when the bus scaled the hill,

chasing one good essential image after you died.
Again, on their course, through shadows contoured as centuries,

the ordinary and marvellous blurred where night fell
while doorways were thrown open to the evening air.

I gathered all I saw even as it fell behind
though what falls behind we gather to give away.

I thought these things while I waited there,
the coast beyond the handrail as far, as near, as fate.

THE MOIRAI

i.m. Elise Partridge (1958–2015)

1

Aboard the hydrofoil to Ischia I remembered
Auden had rented rooms for several summers and wrote

'In Praise of Limestone' there. And, Elise, I thought
of you, in that indirect manner while the local bus lumbered

along its roundabout route through Mezzavia
to Sant'Angelo, bypassing the famed Maronti beaches

where the morning sun dawdles before it reaches
a scorching apex above Mount Epomeo and the view

west that spreads with glintings of the day's turn.
You'd died, your last book done, and because

we'd talked of Auden's work, I searched the terrace-slanted
hills for a 'great good place' where vine, fern,

and bougainvillea delight enough to let grief pause,
and I promised to take nothing for granted.

2

I promised to take nothing for granted,
but near the road's spiny palms, Vespa traffic,

developers' climbing I-beams, and souvenir dreck,
I lapsed in being thankful. What I wanted

felt a fraud, fitting some elegiac notion
into one afternoon, an oath's great *chutzpah*

shaped to honour something sacred. La-di-da.
Yet through the whiff of seaweed and suntan lotion

that followed Ischia's shore, your poems and emails
repeated their elegant lines of gratefulness

and cautioned me in the lucky hours ahead to forgo
the world's cheap shortcuts. Nothing fails

better than the failure to look around. Less
unfocused than spellbound, I'd missed the stop at Forio.

3

Unfocused or spellbound, I'd missed the stop at Forio
where Auden had lived amid flat rooftop gardens

and watchtowers once guarded ports from Saracens.
So I didn't trudge the street, or sip a latte there, for no

greater reason than my head was turned away
when the stop appeared. I would've liked to find,

among the pastel shopfronts, squares, and tree-lined
promenades, a dusty vestige of his stay:

a brass plaque maybe, fixed beside a door frame,
or photograph of his face (gazing discreetly out

from a convivial crowd) left behind and preserved between
bottles on a bar shelf. One trace of him to say 'I came,

I saw, I had a drink.' I continued on our route,
the sky wide and luminous as the Mediterranean.

4

The sky, wide and luminous as the Mediterranean,
kept doing what it does best, being clear

and blue, while we headed north. Each shift of gear
announced the engine's effort, climbing uphill, then

zigzagging down, a tarantella back-and-forth of brake
and rev. In those jolting rhythms, my mind arrived

at a hundred scattered scenes of how I'd lived
that fading year, gutted by the worst of them. Take

the note you'd sent mid-July, requesting edits
for your manuscript (if I didn't mind) with one condition:

diagnosed, you were about to die and needed haste.
Your email bent the air like an earthquake. I read its

desolation. How one word, *terminal*, granted no remission
to the pending days you couldn't count or waste.

The pending days you couldn't count or waste
worked against you while you hurried to compress

each thought, word, and image, into painstaking aptness,
even as you struggled to ignore the pain you faced

through rounds of morphine and chemo. Uncertainty, I guessed,
tried to break your nerve. Your inbox messages

bristled at fatigue, awake at 4 a.m., revising pages
when you could, then sleeping again. That August

and September, I took your poems everywhere I went:
cafes, trains, a bench on Dow's Lake …

Be tough on me, you said, buoyant, your bravado still
polite, apologizing if any replies you sent

were slow, joking at a diet of steroids and cupcakes.
I recalled it all again when the bus scaled the hill.

I recalled it all again when the bus scaled the hill,
watching locals ride as they steadied baskets

of prosciutto and sardines haggled from morning markets.
Others, in an earbud trance, napped until

their stop drew near, then exited, hardly opening
their eyes, to maybe wander into another scene

where any life could change *while someone*
else is eating or opening a window or just walking

dully along, as Auden supposed they might.
The unrehearsed luck we welcome is balanced

by dread, foiling any half-assed guess to what side
fate chooses. Forgive a platitude. It'll sound trite

but at least describes what you were up against,
chasing a good essential image before you died.

7

Chasing a good essential image before you died,
you described Atropos, Lachesis, and Clotho, the three

Greek daughters whose task, on repeat, was to eye
each life up, spin a thread, and decide

the precise length it stretches, where it must end.
What chance do we have against stock figures of grief

carved on tombs and sarcophagi in marble relief?
Even gods submit to their judgement, and pretend

they won't meddle with the fortunes of mortals while
they meddle with them. Homer's heroes learned

there's no knowing which hour one dies, so told stories
to explain away chaos and make the fear simple.

I knew nothing could, as the bus turned
again on its course, through shadows contoured as centuries.

Again, on its course, through shadows contoured as centuries,
the bus braked. At a hillside stop, afternoon

was trickling west beyond the Gulf of Naples, and soon
the rooftop antennae and wind-shook pine trees

would be dispossessed of day. Thinking I was close
to port and could walk the distance back, I exited

into a leafy piazza where the late sun fled
across a church's face, swirls of violins and oboes

drifting from its nave, ending a remembrance mass.
Grandmothers in black stood and genuflected

under triumphant images of Christ the King. (We tell
our stories too). The ornate panels of stained glass

proclaimed miracles. Outside, dusk collected.
The ordinary and marvellous blurred where night fell.

The ordinary and marvellous blurred where night fell.
Beyond the causeway, pleasure boats bobbed, tethered

near the groping headland that gathered
pleats of sapphire sequins from the tide's swell,

then scattered them in sea-spray. The cliff sides
were gowned like Auden's limestone, rounded and porous.

They shone as metaphor, an image he left for us
to show how our public self hides

its subterranean life. Amid change
and something unchanging, I raised my camera to preserve

a remarkable view, knowing they were everywhere
and unsaveable. The Neapolitan sky, soaked in orange

and red, shook in hues above darker surf
while doorways were thrown open to the evening air.

Doorways were thrown open to the evening air,
starting *la passeggiata*. Near a cafe's folded umbrella

I watched families with strollers greet *la bella
serata*, straying aimlessly through the poky square.

Distracted, I'd forgotten Ischia's starker outlines
implied the hour was getting late, and final

departures for Naples left shortly from the terminal.
There was no bus in sight, no road signs

to confirm the distance or direction. I traced steep
hairpins down where traffic mirrors bent

fish-eye views of the descending road vined
in broken light. Elise, I was trying to keep

my vow. Half-running, I had meant
to gather all I saw even as it fell behind.

11

To gather all I saw even as it fell behind
I scanned the harbour, parsing every crest

and trough of surf, like stressed and unstressed
syllables scribbling the tide's cursive, underlined

by a sudden shore. The art you preferred
was that turn of sounds under pressure to make

an elusive music. Language for pleasure's sake
is the ear's best reward, and no word

works the intellect without the beauty of its riff.
I'll hope to shape a decent phrase

to honour what you loved. Hard to say
or guess why and how, when and even if

a poem starts, but I'd argue it's a need to praise.
What falls behind we gather to give away.

What falls behind we gather to give away.
We're here. We're not. It's all we're promised.

No consolation prize or midlife bucket list
might be counted beyond a simple day

of textbook weather. Numb spectators to your courage,
we felt helpless, left to shake a fist

at the attendant Fates, or the harried, kind oncologist
who, like Lachesis, portioned out each page

of the calendar you were leaving. No tidy myth
will console our scattered grief, but since we grieve,

let me send this postcard from a darkened pier,
grateful for how it gave me space to chat with

you again, messages I know you won't receive,
though I thought these things while I waited there.

Though I thought these things while I waited there,
announcements cued me with the sunburnt throng

to cross the gangway for departure, hurried along
by the clacking canter of suitcase wheels, water

roiling where the bollards held the stern. I know
time is always short, whether one day

or a year. Call us back, let us stay,
we beg each better hour. Soon, the *mezzogiorno*

would release my footsteps from its cobbled stones,
count its euros, and see my scuffed luggage

off with an elegy's keepsakes, whatever weight
the allowance can bear. No change of time zones

will erase a loss, no stories or poet's language,
the coast beyond the handrail as far, and near, as fate.

14

The coast beyond the handrail was as far, and near, as fate,
that fancy word for the hours we get, the good,

the bad, the unfair or not. I'm sure you'd
pen a rough draft on that, laugh and berate

yourself for not writing sooner. You'd always write.
Mailed in postmarked manila, those sheets you left behind

I flatten and reread again to find
the outlines of another fate where you might

have survived. How to use the circumstance
of who you are? Friends, family, and your beloved Steve

would say the question's answered
by the way you lived. You honoured time with eloquence

and wonder. You noticed things and praised. I believe
it was aboard the hydrofoil to Ischia that I remembered.

3

The wire fence, the shrub, the edge of the rock garden
seep through soft snow, like developing polaroids.
Out my workroom window, the shed looks picturesque

and weighted. The Queensway is hell.
Rush hour starts at two-thirty. Buzzing the guardrails,
brake lights don't dazzle, but drip like IVs
into the long coma of Kanata. A green stack

masses on radar. Folk music laments
dead animals. Unshaven, I type and delete, push the lines
together, hoping for friction, a habanero heat,
a Hail Mary of dynamite. It's usually domestic;

the afternoon's dishes. The dentist warns, but my teeth
grind all night. The brain won't stop, feet feeling for
the stairwell. Moonlight silvers its rented white walls.

I WALK DRIPPING FROM A SEA JOURNEY ON THE HIGHWAY ACROSS AMERICA IN TEARS TO THE DOOR OF YOUR COTTAGE IN THE WESTERN NIGHT

In sweat-wicking Lycra
I keep afloat on plastic sludge, make landfall
in the bleed of light pollution. I watch
for smoke and skate the remains
of the Keystone XL half-pipe.
The end caps we use for beer steins,
the flare-stacks our tiki torches.
I am post-millennial, post-X, -Y, -Zed,
post-economy, post–black
rhino and –polar bear. I'm now
and only here to party.

•

No Wi-Fi, I jones for fresh apps,
fraught and swiping
the touchscreen for any old download.
I pocket-dial your landline and leave a three-
minute message of trash talk, broken up
                by fabric scrubbing the mic.

It's a prayer from the wastes of the cotton-mouthed
and tongue-tied.
I apologize. I'm packed up tight
and should be upright
and solid as a BILLY bookcase
but there's no Allen key.

•

I'm the West and the East.
Mostly the West, but
                    east of there.
I can dream.
I'm a shopping mall of desire and regret,
trying to buy what
they've got left
before someone else gets their hands on it,

excess of the capitalist carcass,
non-compostable trash
of the factory outlet.
I won't miss out. I'm all
want.
I'm the voice that complains
but will not make the sacrifice.

•

I'd like to improve my life.
I crave Doritos
and fall asleep.
I wake super hungry.
The dawn is a gold bar
on the breezeblocks.
I saw the most bored
minds of my generation,
            so I hired a life coach who red-
flagged my goals. Tom Cruise, save us!
Please jump from a rotor-damaged

and burning chopper
into the U.N. building
through an impossibly narrow air duct
and stop all the complacency, thank you.

You have the secret codes, like this poem.

I'm with you in L.A.,
where you transform our notions of democracy
into box-office gold.
You glide past,
a stylish tatter of crewneck, hooded
leather, and denim,
but around here it's just normcore.
I'm sorry for all the atrocities
and ecosystem collapse. We'll try
better next time.
[Fist-bump] I'm out.

ORBIT

Silverfish swarmed the sugar bowl, fridge
empty, skinny mattress on the hide-a-bed.
Lack's best lived in the past. Working class. Who'd

find the poetry there? Truth is everyone's trying
to get above it, the basement and the bank account.
Walking down steep streets in early evening,
I was glad to be back, jingling my keys and quarters.

Everything was going to be great
until the doom set in. It sleeps in our veins.
It wobbles in orbit decay. An hour free
on a split shift, I shuffled through the vintage wear

and faded LPs. Since I first got here, the highway's
been renamed three times. I open the gate
and stand among the graves, owning nothing.

YEARBOOK

i. (belated) m.: Maryanne Yakabuski (1967–1984)

Straight brown bangs with silver sheen, voice
like a crow, you guarded a desk by the wall in the tough
early teens of the early eighties. Maryanne, we teased

you. Our generation, bullied, bullying, oblivious
to its own cruelty, paid misery forward, the petty
to the poorer. Life kept starting, flawed, groping
for beauty, not deserving of trust, not even

a great haircut. I found the obit again, your face
framed by clouds in a yearbook's slanted sun-rays.
Meanwhile: Madonna, *Back to the Future*, and Live Aid.
Mulroney and Reagan singing 'Irish Eyes.' Nineteen

eighty-five. Gone the most popular of us, the cafeteria
grease, the home-team scores, Prince,
and Bowie. Maryanne, who thinks of you?

The frame of a shop front,
          flashing acetylene white.
Terror lopes into the bolting crowd

flushed out by the sudden violence.
          Hard question marks
                    scythe the commuters' routine, metal shards

like a thresher chawing
the skyline, ripping a hole
          through Wednesday.

Us and Them bow down
below our heaven.

•

TVs broadcast ruin.
          Mortars on the balcony.
                    Dushkas mounted on minivans.

Impact
rolls pancakes of pulverized
          cement powder. Camps

claim the border,
          razor-wire swarming a berm.
The noise keeps mounting,

> a crunching thunder honed

in crosshairs

asking *what*
> *do we save?*

•

Too late
.the answer
before we vanish.

•

How quick our cool hands get hot inside the quarrel;
our outrage, our revenge,

nowhere at the bottom
> of the rain-filled crater, or near the clearing sky.
Nowhere between a cold floor

and the euphoric dash to safety.

Groping at the cut-and-dry, dogma
> of where, when, what we were
and wanted, livid
> with justification,

too far,
too near to hear the nuance
as we fan each Zippoed rag.

Sleeping on the floor, no curtains, waking to a view
of Rue Sainte-Catherine beyond the fire escape.
The sky faded to stars, the rooflines to streetlights.

No shower, but a claw-foot to soak in. Each iron jolt
of a bird-cage elevator clattered the scissor doors.
Beside a basement furnace and three Maytag dryers,
the janitor's apartment was tropical-muggy.

He showed me his oils nailed to the kitchen wall –
still-life studies of bananas and a quart of Labatt's 50 –
while his uncle sang to opera records through the doorless bedroom.
Nothing swept or mopped, no repairs. Exposed walls

and loose wiring amid rumours of the class-action lawsuit.
With new management, the janitor got chucked
by Christmas. Or was it the night before? Twas.

WHIR

Jobless on the half-rotten porch, pulpit
to a sunken trans-Vancouver bike path a minute's
whir from East Hastings. Aimless, couch-

surfing castaway, I thought
youth the best refusal and the great hope.
Jeff obsessed over how a spider gets its web
across the considerable distance between rail post

and magnolia. He asked me. I couldn't say. So went
to the library. Without design, the future shrugged.
I hoped I might find myself over there and not
be disappointed. Identity's alarm. Mere puzzles

juggled when I passed the grim ranks of homeless.
And learned the strand dangles
on the breeze until it sticks to something solid.

I ARRIVE TOO LATE SO WATCH THE FOOTAGE OVER FROM THE BEGINNING

Lost in the sea.
        Battered by the sea.
Calling from the sea

        over a satellite phone.

•

The sea with its marble turmoil.
The sea with its slagheap shimmer.

•

The safe house / Toyota exhaust in darkness /
        the smugglers' grunts /
And also,

also the sea
        to be pushed about toward / crammed on a flatbed toward /
told to keep those children quiet toward /

speechless toward the beaches.

        And ship parts grind above the pitching span,
miles offshore boiling fuel coughing acrid black into below-zero
    dawn,
        the dinghy reek

as you shiver in the sunrise
      in sight of a blue boat with a white line running down its side.

•

The sea teething the hull.

The sea's suck a vacuum grinding the rust for a breach.

The sea's fringed blows shaking breakers toward the shingle.

•

And back there,
      and behind: rockets and cluster bombs
smashing the trauma wards /

      back there,
rations of bread, tomato paste, and lentils /

children huddled in basements

      by the last generators /

      near campfires of furniture /

      behind sniper screens made from torn bedsheets.

•

And beyond the sea,
      your mind shapes foreign words:

train station /
western Europe /
the border

With grief before dawn.

•

With hope before dawn.

•

Now the bail bucket through a chain of hands is tipped over
    gunwales.
        Now dawn rigged with trapped heat scorching the frail,
who,
        green
with delirium, splashed in vomit from the waves' kick and fuel
    fumes,
        legs scrunched
numb from a night-long wait wedged between neighbours,

        are winched up a rope ladder they are too weak to climb.

Now

faces: one or two in tears,
        many smiling, some with songs, some
blinking through the deep open hatch with mylar blankets, hands

thrust to the rushing sky.

Limbs picked over for damage and disease, mouth
        swabbed in triage as bodies are combed from the hold near
dumps of discarded life vests,
E. coli /
head lice /
makeshift tarpaulin tents
        slapped across scrubland

shook awake on a damp mattress under leaking plastic,
        riot police and armies waving clubs near razor-wire,

all that way

to eat some grapes Khalid picked from a nearby farm,
consigned inside the backlog
        of claimants,
with a pair of mismatched shoes, a towel,

and a sleeping child.

I EAT THE LUSCIOUS PALM DATES NEAR AQABA

I'm told the air
is sweet in the factory.

      While the sorting belt
hums, they're hand-packed

into cardboard trays, sealed
under shrink wrap.

•

We're waved
through traffic cones to a safety checkpoint.
                           Police
with semi-automatics strapped
over Kevlar

distribute gifts
of three plump Medjools:
a Ramadan road tactic
          to reduce
drivers' speed near sundown.

•

Hazim's young,
wants better work
than steering tourists
         through the sacred

wastes of Wadi Rum.
I know that look, the small-town
disquiet,
      handcuffed
to the wrists of the future.
He stirs sage tea in a stone pot, checking
his Muslim Pro app
      for the cue to break today's fast.
The sun smears the outcrop
with bands of fire on shadow.

•

By the last hour of light, we
follow the dusty crust
      of desert floor
in a Bedouin 4×4, gather twigs
      and dry grass for kindling,
the sandstone landscape a sound stage of Mars.

It's good to find a cool place
out of the baked sand, where shade
buoys silence,

where the red and green
      strands of our thinking
can be threaded and seamed.

•

We eat. We drink tea.
Then Hazim slugs water,
                    looking shattered.

His scrub-fire grinds into ash.

He walks off, humming the private riffs
                    of being near his God,
to scrape the hunger of an invocation
through the roomy horizon

and hurry his spirit
                    out of this scorched wind.

DECADE

L.A., after Rodney King. The nineties,
same as every other decade,
too early for progress, too late for change.

We worked the breakfast shift groggy. A flattop
of egg and meat sizzled while regulars shuffled
fat newspapers. Hungry for experience,
property was laughable. Obsessing over RE/Search

and Acker books on balconies with acid-wash skylines, push-
button phones, yoga still weird, friends monogamish.
We walked everywhere; it was like a sickness, our pre-
taxi lives. Nights past four, five. Whenever.

I fell in love, inarticulate with awkwardness and Eros.
Wedged between Tiananmen Square and Columbine,
what did anyone hope for. The ashes answer.

I ARRIVE TOO LATE SO WATCH THE FOOTAGE OVER FROM
THE BEGINNING

A plastic bottle in the western desert
        now clawed and chawed and riddled
looks a husk
but still won't decay for a hundred – *hundreds of* – years,
        something like a whack
of a long time

to conclude as micro shard in watermelon
        or swallowed by a tourist and shat into the luxury
toilet
of those once-profitable dried-up Dead Sea hotels,
        flushed from the digestive tract
in an eventual descent

to the seabed.

•

Conclude as lodged in the airpipe of a pelican
        glubbed down its throat pouch.
Reused for microfilament fishing line

        that will garrot a cormorant until it chokes.

Beached
            beside hermit crab and marine iguana
        and crumbling to toxic pellets in the food chain,

amassing like waves onto slick sea grass,

•

a littered delta, slough
of lamination, foam trays, chip bags, plastic water/
Coke bottles/
        and packaging
heave their translucent inventory

where
foam's white piping outlines/
tightens/
        unspools the mid-ocean's fetch

with microbeads its
trillion filings
        and plastic six-pack rings

where a hawksbill turtle struggles in a ghost net, forelimbs
tangled in nylon,

starved with a supper of single-use container,

the albatross with a bottle cap and lighter
        found among its bleached bones, two
plastic straws twisted in its gizzard,

our brief stay noted in a finch's Jurassic eye.

RAW

i. (belated) m.: Kathy Acker (1947–1997)

To arrive like Kathy, no invitation, ripped
jeans, distressed leather, charging past the bouncer
and over a table to hug the party's host. Transgression

means nothing without ejection. Escape to Paris, London,
the ghosts of Times Square; Gold's Gym and trash cans
of the Lower East Side worried her back to San Francisco.
What is taboo? What is influence but imposition? Are we so tired

of ourselves? *If there's any civil war around here, it's identity.*
Writing is crime. The body a hoodlum, in exile
on islands of desire and resistance. Famous, her layovers
lasted months, overstaying on friends' couches, refusing

chemo, last days with vitamins, antioxidants, Chinese teas
and Demerol, letters and notebooks crammed with the raw,
conflicted mind. Torment, not boredom, is the essence of love.

ALBUM

Because Talk Talk is post-rock.
Because Fela Kuti is Afrobeat.
Because Sun Kil Moon is slowcore.

Because Snail Mail is bedroom pop auteur.
Because Ride is shoegazing.
Because Bratmobile is riot grrrl.
Because Public Enemy is hip-hop.

Because Bad Bunny is Latin trap reggaeton.
Because Weyes Blood is lo-fi freak folk.
Because St. Vincent is art-pop avant-funk.
Because Merzbow is noise scene.

Because Son Volt is alt-country.
Because Dizzee Rascal is grime.
Because Shonen Knife is pop punk.

Because Joy Division is dark wave.

I SWIM THE SAME WATERS THE GREEK ARMY ONCE CROSSED

On one side is life, and life

is on the other.

I approach where catkins draggle in clumps
and double, an image perfumed
                              and reversed
on the current's surface.

I was lost in the limestone heights.
I was being brought down
on a hairpin,
slumped against the armrest, snacking
dried apricots while
the driver chucks
pistachio husks into the sun's exhaust.

•

Rest the world here, where it slows.
Enter the same river three times.
Midges fuzz the waterline, and cloud
a dawdling bend.
With the engine stopped,
                        the horizon
tricks us out of thinking
every delay's an awful thing.

The light's just right for this.

•

I prod my soul and push my soul
but it never complies. I speak to it sometimes
and say

I was the worst at being near you.

Maybe it tarries in ports
where I rested on my way to déjà vu.
But blue shadows, and lapped hulls,
might not bother us.

•

Below Lycian tombs,
a staircase slips into the sea,
no threshold
                    at either end.
The distorted anchor
and sunken ruins levitate in shakings
of turquoise.
Damselflies malinger in scrub oak,
roost in verbena, hover near tamarisk.

I wade into shallows, steadied
by saplings, my heels frenching
suck-holes of mud,

stride the swab of rotting fern
where each ripple burps
a silt cloud,
                    ankles
spangled with bowed daylight, brushing
antiquity's rust and crumbled capstones.

•

The afternoon opened

and a thought became where
we should go.
So now I've cannonballed to bottom, immersed,
hugging naked knees, a cold
splash at the end of one long flight

and several roads,
                    heat gone, the sky

a magnified glass above shore grass
where the core can't
hide in a boat's wake, where
the sea,
all hacksilver and tinsels,
twists inside its braids.

4

SINK

When I thought I was going to die, I did
the dishes. Side plates first, I lined them up at one end
of the rack, then tackled cups, bowls, and forks,

each stain and crumb rinsed until the soap drained
off. Background was fridge hum and TV Ontario.
A panel lamented bark damage wrought by
the invasive ash borer. Infomercial, celebrity bio. A lot

of coke and fun, lifestyles get bonkers
while the young are exultant and impatiently loved.
A porch screen pixelates the breezy outdoors. On Giveaway
Weekend, our curb's a real dump. Hard pass on the greasy

toaster; dibs on the pipe wrench. Oh, to be back
in the car with the ultrasound over, the lump a hematoma.
When the sink sucks the suds, it's thunder.

HORIZON

They had left a row of tulips along the pathway
when we came. Each year, though the soil was moved,
fine yellow blooms poked through the grass.

A wind would bluster, banging at the eaves,
thundering like a box collapsing down some stairs.
It wasn't Greece. Not Italy. But the day could bend
across the walls in a ballroom waltz of sun. Archives

won't record each moment a door closed, a kettle
boiled, each call with sudden news, bad
or good. We watched the horizon arranged outside
our care. After the fire, our bamboo blinds

lay blackened in the ashes. The illusions
fall away. *Two days from now tomorrow
will be yesterday.* It feels like I just got here.

OTHERWISE

Today, I'd even postpone my procrastination
to find some breathing space to consider how
best to squander wasted hours. It's a conflict

of disinterest. There's always something less to do
before what should be happening otherwise.
I thrive in the surplus, steeping like pekoe. It might be
okay to take a time-out, hang back, to rubberneck

the world's accident and let some
other less-than-innocent bystander persist
with the Jaws of Life. It's nice here where there's
nothing to do, paused on a pillow, provisional

as the rosetta hue on this bedroom wall. Showered,
I dress and coast through the hallway onto the street.
I think the memory-foam has already forgotten me.

I PARK THE CAR AND CLIMB THREE FLIGHTS OF STAIRS
for William O'Meara (1935–2014)

In this pantomime of normal: ticking
engine, the numbered
stub on the dash,
branches profiled with hospital
light poles.
      I cross the lot
to your bedside, halfway through
the pop-up book
of my ad hoc adulthood.

•

You listen while we talk, gaunt
above the bright Jell-O. I touch
your head, tough brow
beneath my hand,
      your torso stitched as a railyard.

Eyes hole-punched in bone
organize me through morphine.

Whatever I passed en route, I return to you,
the highway and its rumble-strips,
its passing lanes,
      the trucker chat
at gas stop counters.

I would have brought the oil can,
the red rags flagging lumber,

and removed
this pain and Purell waft

here by your last window.

•

Cafeteria off-hours
glow in LED,
the soft spaceship-hum of something vended,
                              a helix-
rack of day-old muffins
and fruit cups

turning in my view.

•

Don't die too much right now
near the oxygen mask and bendable straws.
Among the nurse's shuffling shoes,
elevator doors skate
a monotonous, machine-cut
groove.

Among the laundry bags
stuffed with sterile gowns,
voices, faces,
          and family anecdotes.

•

We idle in the dark together. Our thoughts
are loose wires in separate walls
lulled by the huff of an ECG.
Me near the armour of your grasping hand.
You, draped in the raiment of these
late minutes, your face a cameo
resting on the pillow.
I watch each breath lift

                    and fall, the self

a sand-shape
picked away by tide.

•

As much as possible
I picture you behind the wheel, your eye
scanning new subdivisions,
ditches dozered from the grass
along new concession lines,

or again
inspecting the thermometer
in the burnished a.m.
at one end
of the kitchen table.

•

Over the fields of baled hay.

•

As much as possible
in the first snows.

The future is needy.

Last week
it wanted what this week
is background,

patchy developments yet to come.
Carry me around, I said,

fetal in the duvet.

Outside, I pause below
clouds feigning menace on radar,
the air dark and radiant
as a nave in Sainte-Chapelle.

•

A short climb to domestic views.
The sky jams the tree in its scrapbook.
One branch, a witch's finger,
scrapes the metal siding,

its impromptu signal keening in wind.
I push tumbled twigs about,
the hibernated slurry,
                leaves, dust,
and litter's dregs, disassembled
fractions

of something whole we used
and threw away.

New stalks breach rolls of soil
like a burst couch.

●

My porch. My staff and straw.
My six treads
down.
My peninsula amid compost bins,
sidewalk, chrysanthemum, and linden, this
provisional mount to my works
and days, each plan
a false trail
where I play a poor man's Hesiod

left to wait
in this shoe-gazer's almanac
remade by the age
of Big Oil and Plastic.

●

Panic lives in my ear,
plus the radio

and a revving at the stop signs.

I shift the piles, spray the lids,
curse drudgery,

but out here free at least
from click-bait. A squirrel's eye
flickers over would-be
predators, if only to outlive
the imminent, heavy rain.

The past, with its exhausted magic,
needs us too.

All facade, the gutters drip
and a Google search shows nothing.

I step toward the porch
and hold the storm between shattered
blades of light.
A predicted front
will pass this way yet completely startle,

and this day will have me for its dinner or let me go.

DER IRISCHE DICHTER MATTHEW SWEENEY IST TOT

for Matthew (1952–2018)

Was that you I heard howling near a lilac hedge

on Sunday morning? You claimed you'd been
a dog in a past life, and insisted public readings
were all the better if one were present.

Also good food, Bordeaux, some creaky jazz,
and a rucksack of fibs. Is a lie still called a cod
in Ireland? You said one day you'd give me a proper

tour of Donegal, where we'd pull up to a bar
with all its windows facing the sea. At least
I knew what enormous fun it was to sit

and laugh at your stories about the lighthouse
and dancing bear. Did the bear
dream the dog, or did the dog dream the bear?

The sea dreamt you.

If we're going to swing back here sometime, we need
to rush away. No gain poormouthing the hometown;
no loss getting the hell out of there. Expect bad

advice, wrong turns, a comeuppance, three a.m. dread of
no God, or was that just the curried onion? One evening we woke
from jetlag to views of palm-lined fields and a salt-trace
of coast. I wavered on the sultry balcony. I was in danger

of getting wise to something outside the dizzy
fear of being. Then the real downpour; the sky's plangent
shudders and a type of rain that floated thresholds.
I had one pair of hiking shoes you likened to loss

of agency, but it was just shit planning. When the self
loosens, it rattles. What we couldn't do, we kept imagining.
The wet drained off us; we got dry and changed socks.

DAYS

We keep forgetting something back there, don't we?
We pop out the door, turn corners, the shops unchanged,
but data nags like a black box has signalled

from the wreckage, or a high voice is calling down
a long street across medians of statued piazzas,
river bends, concert halls (vertigo in the nosebleeds), barista
beardos at homogeneous counters, X-rayed luggage,

passport please, carousel fatigue, caffeinated reveries in taxis,
the balcony's very non-sea view, our frugal mattress picnics
watching own-goals in stoppage time, the must-sees we didn't, phone
calls, emails, our return's fine-toothing of apartment vacancies

with thoughts that nothing would change, as if we'd rush back
through traffic, across three continents, a decade, to find
my father still alive, the cat at its bowl, and the iron left on.

I SLEEP AS THE VOLCANO ASH FALLS LIKE SNOW

Reader, my theme
is boredom and mystery.

First I lean on the counter, then sign the guestbook.

I drink cans of Asahi
on a pine bench in the backpacker's hostel
while dusk sucks
terrain into a fish-lens background.

Later, my patience frets
on the hard bunk,

because the earth is knotted pottery on a crimson storm

and I can't start my life.

•

Sentient fleck under a satellite's flight path,
I twist and dream on a futon.
I turn night's reverie on a hot spit

while a racoon loots the bins.
Fears drift
over clay tiles and gingko, weightless it seems
until the roof sags.

I'm in the middle of this, whatever this is.
Equidistant to breakfast and the darkness behind, balanced
in what I mean by eternity.

•

Over rice in the Kyushu kitchen,
the student
described how his parents met:
a Japanese woman healing
an American's chronic pain with acupuncture
after his Suzuki dropped and buckled,
dragging
the footpeg off its frame, hot manifold
on pavement where

his hip peeled through denim
across the slate of the turn,
the atrophied joints coerced from smashed
limbs

into gesture.

•

I'm what, twenty-three?
Twenty-four?
I can't start my life. I'm coarse, petulant. Green
as wasabi, I can't tell the student
the story
of bumpy latitudes ahead

or the death of both our fathers.

•

Do some thinking now.

A pause will cloud cut glass.

In this story, where do we go?
Who lives, who dies?

Ridiculous.

Not where, how. Not how,
when.
Our luck might outlast the chemo, a storm surge,
a bumped stress-point on an airplane's wing.

One hand surrenders, another takes,
and there's reckless skidding,
a buzzsaw of sparks

before the tally of internal damage.

•

Inside my mind:

wet fields,
the train window,
the elegant hiragana
on fence slats.

A caldera's curve in mist
like a steaming bowl of miso.

•

It's almost dawn.

Strip-lit,
eggshell-white, the ceiling waits
above the spotless tatami.
My father backs his truck from the garage,
the dog we loved

races through tall grass

and disappears into the whispering hillside.

Is life going to happen?
Does it start there, or just
there? We stall, halfway
between our arrangements and unravelling.

Maybe the student died, outlived
by his parents.
He'd only paused near me
for an hour north of Kumamoto,
and twenty-five years later,

just a walk-on in a dream.

We might have slept for years, extras in each other's grief.

Dear reader, I misled you.

Back there
the ash keeps falling.

Midnight shoulders each memory's weight

while the sleeping lanes ring with echoes.

LISBON

At the Rinaldo-owned hotel, his career highlights
loop on the elevator wall; canned cheering coruscates
down the switchback stairs. A Greek god worms
through his smirk, oblivious to hubris or change.

Triumphal arch is shade from noon. On steep flagstones
toward the Crusade ramparts, my middle-aged
throbbing shins track the Middle Ages. To wake

from a nap, lower back balky, grey hair in the razor
and around the modish sink. Cartilage crackles. I feel mortal
as a suckling pig, but not as rich. Is this headache
just the vinho verde, the LBV, the trudge through Alfama?

Is it too late to make this a love poem? I just got here
and barely two lines left. Your form moves
in slatted light, the best years saying *follow me.*

I TRAVEL

If I were told I would have to go,
then I would very much
like to stay.

No mystery thriller this,
but the trail dries up
as the evidence amasses.

•

Even when it isn't, isn't it
always the weather?

There is always the sky
viewed through a square.

•

I was hoping to own
what I gathered around me.
Like any ticket, it was not
the event
but a guaranteed entry I needed.
Not what I saw,
but how it received me,

wild, immense,
and muted

like a snowstorm on the ocean.

•

There's the noise and buzz of going there.

So I rushed the stage.
Because I don't want to wait here
waving my arms.

I'm still. That's how it feels.
I wait all winter for the animal to die,
raise its chin, look
into time. I
lack the south and Lord Tequila. I wonder
where good comes. Here in my head
I'm a litter of one, and I rage, slosh unease like brine.

•

Mid-life, I waver at the sink
amidst a hacking cough and hurt the more the cure
recedes. I was on the bottom
of the upswing. I wanted boost. I set the pails
for use and kept a long flow.
But I meant to climb, have wanted
every passerby to slow and pause
and be a mirror.

•

Sometimes nature's wrong. Look at the runt I saved!
Look how each selection
is *because* of love. Ground down,
look how gravel
becomes a beach.

What did I choose?

I tend the meadow, take
pains like everyone,

play the numbers against the grief.

•

I huff the ducts of burning dust, and dream
a hot gulf.
I'm home, low-ceilinged. I too
would grow an avocado, my wooden core
a seed.

•

In its defence, the year's sprawl
is skulked by any piece of news.

I walk blocks, side-
step a young couple unloading groceries
for the newborn, with ginger steps,
still surprised,
like volunteers inside an earthquake.
Tacking left,

I clutch a bundle of spirit
and breath.

•

The river was easy. The cold, not.
It's how we lied

that we kept things safe.

I raise the animal on creaky limbs
and nudge the water bowl.
I post the notes, I check
the links, new forecasts, catalogues, and results
and think it best to think far less
about those things.

And rummage the vintage shops for tin.

'I Surf the Sodium Light': search 'Town of Cobourg Fox & Owl Video' on YouTube.

'I Replace Korotki at the Weather Station on the Barents Sea' was inspired by a photo essay by Evgenia Arbugaeva in the *New Yorker*.

'The Moirai': My friend Elise Partridge and I continued an irregular correspondence via real letters – and some emails – between the four or five face-to-face visits we had over the years, all kept lively with various commentaries and discussions on poetry, particularly that of W. H. Auden. In the summer of 2014, Elise contacted me with the devastating news she had been diagnosed with cancer. Elise had beaten breast cancer already (documented in her second book, *Chameleon Hours*) but this one, colon cancer, was terminal. With this email was a request that I edit her final book, accepted by House of Anansi Press for the following spring. What followed were several months of intense emailed discussions and edits, resulting in Elise's *The Exiles' Gallery*. Throughout hospital bouts, chemo sessions, meetings with her estate lawyer, and a last trip for New Year's Eve in Times Square with her husband, Stephen, Elise was steadfast in her commitment to craft and quality. Enduring discomfort and pain, she was able to see the manuscript through final proofs and a cover design before she died on January 31st, 2015, a few weeks short of the book's publication date. Her poem 'Fates,' included in that collection, was the last to be added to the manuscript. The narrative of 'The Moirai' occurred the following year.

The title 'I Walk Dripping From a Sea Journey on the Highway Across America in Tears to the Door of Your Cottage in the Western Night' is adapted from the final line of Allen Ginsberg's *Howl*.

'Raw': The italicized phrase in line 8 is from *In Memoriam to Identity* by Kathy Acker.

'Horizon': Italicized lines (13–14) are quoted from *These Are Not the Potatoes of my Youth* (Goose Lane Editions, 2019) by Matthew Walsh.

THANKS AND SALUTATIONS

Some of these poems appeared in earlier versions in the following publications: *Arc Poetry Magazine, RiddleFence, Southword Journal, Hazlitt, The Walrus, Brick: A Literary Journal,* and *Galaxy Brain.* Much thanks to the tireless efforts of their editors and all the administrators, publishers, editors, festival directors, associates, board members, magazine committee members, coordinators, teachers, funding-application sloggers, librarians, arts volunteers, and fellow practitioners of art for saving the world each day with advocacy for, and the protection of, wild and expansive thought.

Thank you:

For financial support provided through the Canada Council for the Arts, the Ontario Arts Council, and the City of Ottawa during the writing of this book.

To Nick Laird, Gerður Kristný, and Gregory Scofield for their generosity and time.

For permission to use their art, my deep admiration and gratitude to John Minihan and Jan Baracz for, respectively, the author and cover photos.

I'm immensely grateful my book was steered into existence by the generous creative hands of Alana Wilcox, James Lindsay, and Crystal Sikma at Coach House Books.

I'm indebted to the superlative writers Ken Babstock, Barbara Nickel, Harold Hoefle, and Stephanie Roberts, who offered invaluable feedback, support, and profound friendship during this book's progress.

And to my editor, Matthew Tierney, heartfelt gratitude for his committed, meticulous, and inspired work pushing against my clumsy phrases and sending me in far better directions.

Both my parents, William and Dorothy, passed away during the writing of this book. I'm still thinking of what to say. There is another book for them. With love and gratitude.

David O'Meara lives in Ottawa, Canada.

OTHER BOOKS BY DAVID O'MEARA

Storm Still, McGill-Queen's University Press, 1999.
The Vicinity, Brick Books, 2003.
Noble Gas, Penny Black, Brick Books, 2008.
A Pretty Sight, Coach House Books, 2013.

Typeset in Arno and Korolev.

Printed at the Coach House on bpNichol Lane in Toronto, Ontario, on Zephyr Antique Laid paper, which was manufactured, acid-free, in Saint-Jérôme, Quebec, from second-growth forests. This book was printed with vegetable-based ink on a 1973 Heidelberg KORD offset litho press. Its pages were folded on a Baumfolder, gathered by hand, bound on a Sulby Auto-Minabinda, and trimmed on a Polar single-knife cutter.

Coach House is on the traditional territory of many nations, including the Mississaugas of the Credit, the Anishnabeg, the Chippewa, the Haudeno-saunee, and the Wendat peoples, and is now home to many diverse First Nations, Inuit, and Métis peoples. We acknowledge that Toronto is covered by Treaty 13 with the Mississaugas of the Credit. We are grateful to live and work on this land.

Edited by Matthew Tierney
Cover and interior design by Crystal Sikma
Cover photograph by Jan Baracz
Author photo by John Minihan

Coach House Books
80 bpNichol Lane
Toronto, ON M5S 3J4
Canada

416 979 2217
800 367 6360

mail@chbooks.com
www.chbooks.com